·GROWING UP IN·
Aztec Times
MARION WOOD

Illustrated by
RICHARD HOOK

Troll Associates

Library of Congress Cataloging-in-Publication Data

Wood, Marion, (date)
  Growing up in Aztec times / by Marion Wood; illustrated by
Richard Hook.
      p.   cm.
  Includes index.
  Summary: Describes the daily life of the Aztecs, discussing life
in the city, life in the country, education, food and drink, and
other aspects.
  ISBN 0-8167-2723-6 (lib. bdg.)   ISBN 0-8167-2724-4 (pbk.)
  1. Aztecs—Juvenile literature.   2. Aztecs—Children—Juvenile
literature.   [1. Aztecs—Social life and customs.   2. Indians of
Mexico—Social life and customs.]   I. Hook, Richard, ill.
II. Title.
F1219.73.W66   1993
972'.004974—dc20   91-39444

Published by Troll Associates

Design by James Marks
Edited by Kate Woodhouse

Printed in the U.S.A.

10 9 8 7 6 5 4 3 2 1

Contents

The Aztec empire

More than 500 years ago, much of present-day Mexico was ruled by a fierce and powerful people called the Aztecs. The Spaniards who explored Mexico in the early 16th century were amazed by the splendor of the Aztec empire. They decided to attack the Aztecs, who fought fiercely, but in the end the Aztecs were defeated and their wealth seized. Their emperor, Montezuma, was killed and their great city, Tenochtitlán, was demolished. Many Aztecs died in the fighting, or later of hunger and disease.

Some of the Spaniards left descriptions of what they saw. Many objects are preserved in museums, and the remains of buildings have been discovered under the streets of modern Mexico.

◄ The Great Temple in Tenochtitlán was sacred to the gods of war and rain. Stone knives were used by priests to sacrifice people to the gods.

► The pink area of the large map shows the extent of the Aztec empire in Central America under Montezuma, and the location of its greatest city, Tenochtitlán. The map insert shows how the city was linked by causeway to Lake Texcoco.

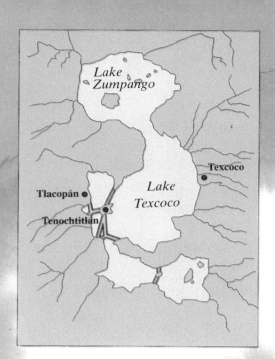

Lake Zumpango

Texcoco

Tlacopán ●

Lake Texcoco

Tenochtitlán

GULF OF MEXICO

● Tenochtitlán

PACIFIC OCEAN

5

Who were the Aztecs?

The Aztecs were not always powerful rulers. Aztec children heard how their ancestors were poor hunters wandering in the deserts of northern Mexico.

The Aztecs reached the Valley of Mexico around 1300. At first they worked for the people already there. Then, according to legend, their god Huitzilopochtli told them to look for a sign—an eagle grasping a snake perched on a prickly-pear cactus. If they settled where they found this sign, they would become rich and powerful.

The Aztecs found the spot described by the god on a swampy island in Lake Texcoco. They built a village of reed huts that they called Tenochtitlán—"the place of the prickly-pear cactus."

▼ The Aztecs constructed their "floating gardens" by spreading mud from the bottom of the lake over bundles of reeds or wicker rafts. They planted trees around the ends of the rafts to anchor them. Most of Tenochtitlán was built in this way.

The Aztecs worked hard. They reclaimed land from the lake by building artificial islands or "floating gardens." These were very fertile and the village prospered. The Aztecs became rich and powerful, just as the gods foretold. They conquered other people in the region and took over their land. This was the beginning of the Aztec empire.

The city of the Aztecs

By 1500, Tenochtitlán was probably the largest city in the world. About half a million people lived there. From a distance it looked as though its towering pyramids and palaces rose from the lake itself. The city was crisscrossed by a network of canals and linked to the mainland by three great stone causeways. Between the whitewashed houses were gardens filled with flowers. There were parks with pools and fountains and a zoo with animals brought from every part of the empire.

The great central square of Tenochtitlán was the hub of the empire, constantly crowded with people going about their daily business. Richly dressed nobles and government officials mingled with tribesmen from distant lands, who were bringing tribute to the emperor. Black-painted priests with long matted hair and cloaks embroidered with human skulls climbed the steps of the temples. Sometimes, to the sound of trumpets, the emperor himself appeared, carried on a litter.

▼ This is Tenochtitlán's central square. All the important ceremonies and festivals were held here.

8

▼ High-ranking warriors wearing wooden headdresses carved to look like eagles or jaguars strode through the crowd.

9

Life in the country

Most people in the empire were farmers. People were usually given some land to farm when they married. There were no sheep, cows, or horses in Aztec times. These were brought to America by the Spaniards in the 16th century. But turkeys were native to Mexico, and there were usually a few scratching outside the farmer's thatched hut. Rabbits and ducks were also bred for food, and bees were kept for honey.

▼ The farmer's main tool was a long stick flattened at one end. This could be used to turn the soil, plant seeds, and pull out weeds.

10

Huge amounts of food had to be produced to feed all the people of the empire. The main crops were corn, beans, squash, amaranth, and chili peppers. Corn was the most important. Aztec farmers grew two corn crops a year, one in spring and another in late summer. Even so, there was often a famine when crops failed or if the grain ran out before the next harvest was ready. It was then the duty of the emperor to supply the people with food from his reserves.

▼ Farmers and all the members of their families worked long hours tending their plots of land.

Inside an Aztec house

Only in the center of Tenochtitlán was the ground firm enough to support stone buildings. Elsewhere in the city, where land had been reclaimed from the lake, people lived in low, flat-roofed houses built of mud bricks.

Poor families often had only one main room, but usually, as people became wealthier, they added more rooms. Many people needed working areas as well as living rooms. Craftsmen, for example, needed workshops, and merchants required storerooms.

▼ Rich people had slaves to wait on them and tend the garden. Slaves were often debtors or prisoners of war.

▼ There was often a separate bathhouse in the courtyard. It was heated and water was thrown in to make steam.

Houses were built around a central courtyard. Here the children could play and the women could spin and sew. People spent a lot of time outdoors, just as they do today in Mexico's hot, sunny climate. Most houses were bordered on at least one side by a canal, and every family had its own landing place.

Inside, houses were rather plain, with whitewashed walls and hard earth floors. Everyone, rich and poor alike, sat and slept on woven reed mats laid on the floor. Clothes and valuables were stored in wicker chests. The palaces of the emperor and the nobles were a little more comfortable, with a few low wooden tables and wicker chairs and perhaps some painted or embroidered hangings to cover the walls.

Everyday life

Everyone rose early, as soon as it was light. Women and girls dressed in loose, sleeveless blouses and skirts. Men and boys wore loincloths, with cloaks knotted on one shoulder. Girls wore their hair loose until they married. Then they pinned it up in braids on either side of their heads.

Ordinary people were allowed to wear only plain garments woven from agave fiber. But those worn by the nobles were of richly embroidered cotton. There were also strict rules about jewelry. Some jewels, such as turquoise nose ornaments, could be worn only by the emperor.

During the day most people were hard at work. The emperor's palace filled up with the many officials who worked there. Farmers went to their fields and craftsmen to their workshops. Traders took their goods to sell at the market. Children went to school, while their mothers prepared meals. After work, people enjoyed playing or watching games. Only nobles were allowed to play *tlachtli*, a kind of basketball. Players tried to hit a rubber ball through a stone ring set high on a wall. It was a rough game and players were often injured, and even killed.

▶ *Patolli* was a popular game rather like Parcheesi. Marked beans were used as dice and colored pebbles as counters.

The birth of a baby

The birth of a baby was a joyful occasion for the whole family. As soon as they heard the news, friends and relatives flocked to visit. They brought special gifts that were meant to prepare the baby for later life. A baby boy was given a miniature shield, bow, and arrows because everyone hoped he would become a brave warrior. A baby girl received a little loom so that she would grow up to be a good wife and mother.

When it was time for the baby to be given a name, the family sent for a soothsayer. This was a priest who had studied the stars and could work out the meaning of the signs under which the baby had been born.

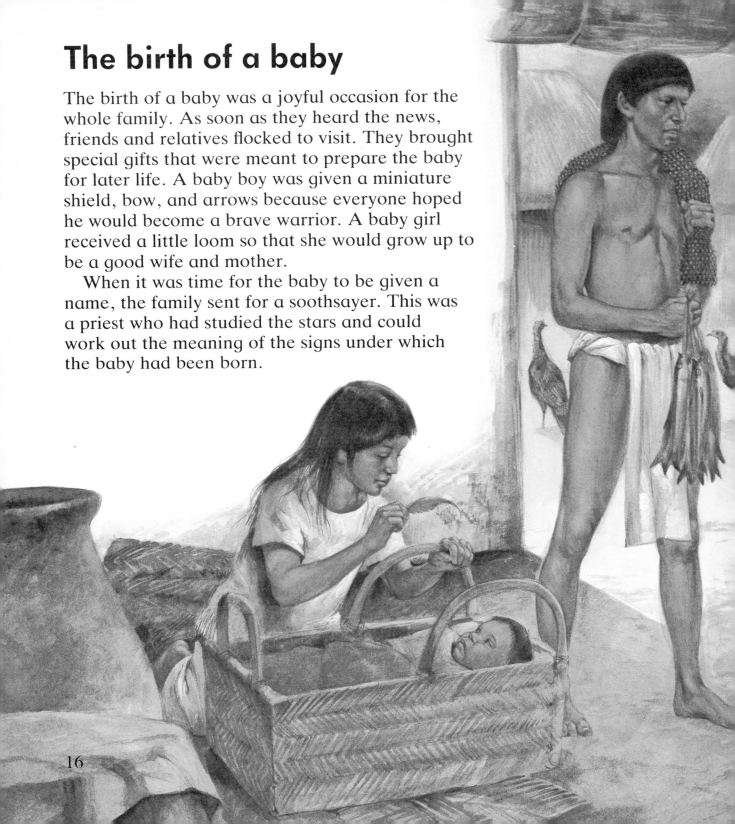

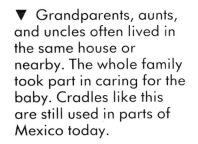

▼ Grandparents, aunts, and uncles often lived in the same house or nearby. The whole family took part in caring for the baby. Cradles like this are still used in parts of Mexico today.

Some signs were considered luckier than others. If the baby had been born on an unlucky day, the naming ceremony would be put off. Usually, babies were named after the day of their birth. Since many babies were born on the same day, each one was also given a special name. Girls might be called Quiauhxochitl (Rain Flower), or Atototl (Water Bird). Boys had names such as Chimalpopoca (Smoking Shield), or Quauhcoatl (Eagle Snake).

Early learning

Aztec children were expected to work hard from an early age. Small children were sent to gather firewood and fetch water almost as soon as they could walk. Older children helped their parents carry heavy loads to and from the market.

Boys often worked alongside their fathers. Farmers' sons helped with the crops. They learned to handle canoes on the lake and helped find food. Their fathers taught them how to catch fish using spears and nets, and how to set snares for water birds. Girls helped their mothers at home.

Aztec parents were fond of their children, but they were strict. Lazy or disobedient children were scratched with thorns or held near a fire of burning peppers to make their eyes sting.

▼ The family of a feather worker helps to decorate a shield with brightly colored feathers. By helping in his father's workshop, a boy soon learned the skills of the craft.

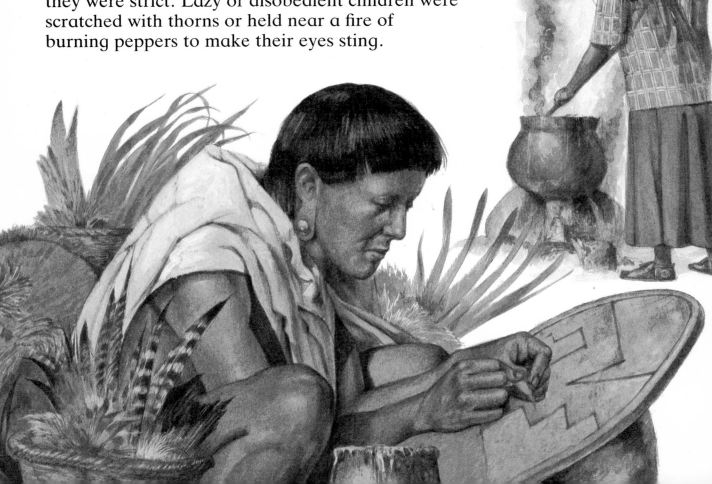

▼ A girl learned to weave by watching her mother. She learned how to spin thread and practiced on little spindles. When she was older, she learned to weave the thread into cloth.

19

At the market

Goods from all over the empire flooded into Tenochtitlán. Every day canoes crowded the lake, carrying their cargoes by canal right into the heart of the city. Merchants often spent years on trading trips to distant and dangerous lands in search of rare or valuable items. Almost everything you might imagine was offered for sale: food and clothing of every kind, pottery, furniture, flint knives and copper axes, paper, and paints.

▼ Merchants sold everything from fruit and vegetables to precious jewels. 60,000 people went to the market daily.

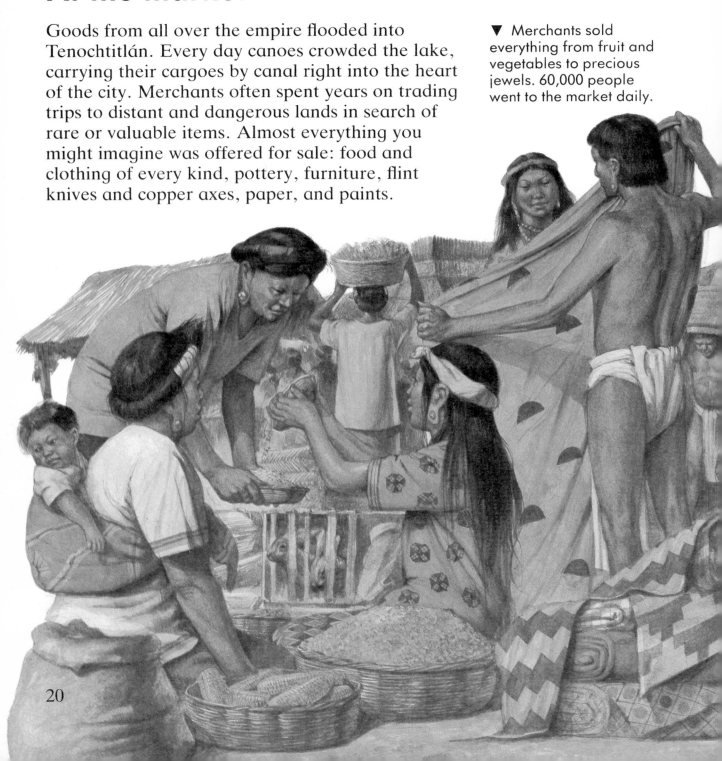

The Aztecs did not use money. People exchanged what they had for what they wanted. Cacao beans or goose quills filled with gold dust were used as small change.

Food and drink

People ate nothing when they got up. They had breakfast around ten o'clock, after several hours' work. This was usually a bowl of corn porridge, flavored with honey or pepper. The main meal was at about midday. For ordinary people, seated on mats around the hearth, the meal was simple. They ate meat only on special occasions. People ate lots of vegetables such as beans, tomatoes, and sweet potatoes. And there were always freshly made *tortillas*, corn pancakes baked on a flat stone over the fire. Everything was washed down with water.

▼ Rich people often gave banquets that lasted all night long. Guests were entertained by musicians, dancers, and acrobats, and given presents of cloaks and flowers.

Meals in a rich household were grander. As well as tortillas, there was turkey, pheasant, duck, deer, wild pig, and rabbit. They ate fish, frogs, tadpoles, shrimps, and Mexican salamanders called axolotls, and drank cocoa, sweetened with honey or whisked into a scented froth with vanilla.

Going to school

All Aztec boys had to go to school, starting when they were about 10 or 12. The sons of rich people were sent to a *calmecac*. This was a boarding school attached to a temple and run by priests.

Here the boys learned to read and write. They studied books on history, medicine, and astrology. The Aztecs did not have an alphabet as we do. Instead they wrote in pictures or *glyphs*. Glyphs were drawn according to strict rules, and a person needed much training to be able to read and write them. Books were made of sheets of bark paper or deerskin folded like an accordian.

◄ The calmecac, or religious school, was very strict. Boys were expected to work hard here. The school trained them to become priests or high-ranking government officials.

Life at the calmecac was not easy. The boys lived on tortillas and water and slept on the bare floor. Several times a night they had to get up to pray or offer incense to the gods. They had to help the priests in religious ceremonies and they worked on the land belonging to the temple. When the boys left school, they could become priests themselves or work as doctors, scribes, or soothsayers.

► Girls did not usually go to school, but some did go to a calmecac and were trained as priestesses or doctors.

25

Training to be a warrior

A *telpochcalli* was a boarding school where boys were trained to be warriors. They were taught to use bows and arrows, swords, and spears. At first they practiced with wooden weapons, and then they learned to use real ones and followed trained warriors into battle. The most fearsome Aztec weapon was the *macahuitl*, a wooden sword edged with sharp pieces of obsidian. Warriors wore padded tunics and carried shields.

It was every young warrior's ambition to take three prisoners alive in battle. He then had the right to tie up his hair in a topknot and wear a feather headdress.

▶ Two boys practice fighting with wooden swords under the watchful eye of an experienced warrior.

▼ The boys at the telpochcalli also had to work in the fields and repair canals and ditches. But they often spent their evenings singing and dancing.

27

Getting married

Boys left the calmecac or telpochcalli to get married when they were about 20. A young man had to marry if he wanted his own house and land.

Marriages were arranged by the young couple's parents. First, they consulted a soothsayer to find out whether the bride and groom were suited. If all was satisfactory, the matchmaker was called in. This was an old woman who acted as a go-between for the two families. Finally, the soothsayer checked that the day chosen for the wedding was a good one.

At nightfall the bride was led to the bridegroom's house by her friends and relations. The young couple sat on mats by the hearth and exchanged presents. The matchmaker tied the young man's cloak and the girl's blouse together, and from that moment they were married.

There are no more Aztec weddings today, because their empire has been gone for hundreds of years. But we will never forget the great civilization they created.

▼ The wedding ceremony was performed by the matchmaker. After the ceremony there was a huge feast with lots of singing and dancing.

Fact file

The Aztec calendar

The Aztecs used two calendars to work out their dates. One calendar was of 365 days divided into 18 "months" of 20 days with 5 extra days at the end. The other consisted of 260 days divided into 13 "periods" of 20 days and was used to foretell the future. The following diagram shows how this second calendar worked.

The wheel on the left has 13 numbers. The wheel on the right has 20 named days. The wheels turn so that each number fits in with a day.

If you begin on 1 Rabbit, the next day is 2 Water and so on. After 13 days the wheel comes around to 1 again. A new period begins on 1 Crocodile.

The Aztecs believed that there were lucky and unlucky days. For example, 1 Serpent was a good day for beginning a journey. Anyone born on 4 Dog was sure to become rich and successful, but those born on 1 Jaguar would die as prisoners of war.

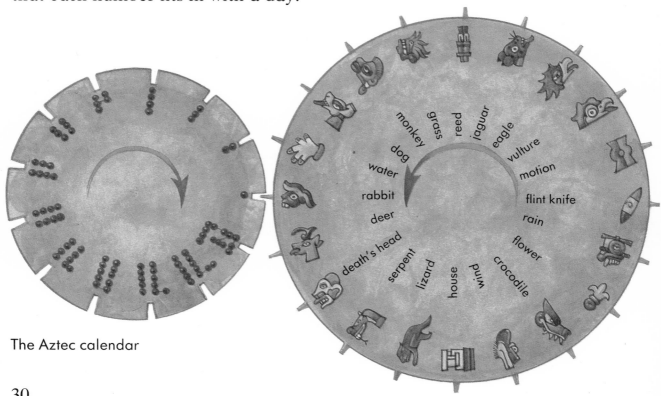

The Aztec calendar

An Aztec book

Writing

As the Aztecs had no alphabet they wrote in the form of little pictures called glyphs. Books were written by priests specially trained as scribes to read and write glyphs. Many Aztec books were about history or religion.

The books were written on the bark of the wild fig tree. The bark was coated with a varnish and stuck together in strips, which could be up to 35 feet (11 meters) long. The artist drew on both sides of the bark and then folded it like a map. The pictures were drawn according to strict rules with important people drawn larger.

In addition to religious and history books, the scribes also kept records of legal decisions and the government lists of the tribute or taxes due to the emperor.

Tribute was paid in the form of goods such as blankets, bundles of feathers, or bags of cacao beans. Pictures of these goods appeared in the tribute lists with the amounts shown by number signs. For instance, 1 was a dot or a finger, 20 was a flag, 400 was a sign like a tree, and 8000 a bag. So the number 8448 consisted of a bag, a tree sign, 2 flags, and 8 dots.

Most of our knowledge of the Aztecs is based on the glyphs and books drawn by the scribes. The glyphs present an interesting and detailed picture of Aztec life.

31

Index